Lewis Clark's field guide to
Wild flowers of the arid flatlands
in the Pacific Northwest

Compiled and photographed by

Lewis J. Clark

Edited and composed by

John G. S. Trelawny, B.Sc.

Design by John Houghton

Gray's Publishing Limited, Sidney, British Columbia, Canada

1 × 0·7

1. MARIPOSA LILY, *Calochortus macrocarpus*

Lavender to pink or white blooms as much as 5″ across, with pointed sepals even longer than the petals, make this species unmistakable. Erect stems up to 20″ high, with thin linear leaves, curled at the tips, bear one or two of these splendid blooms, lifting their beautiful faces upwards. From June to August they grace dry hillsides and benchlands from s. B.C. southward e. of the Cascades on the Columbia Plateau in e. Wash. and Ore., and s. to n.e. Cal. This is the most widespread of the Mariposa Lilies, but it suffers much from grazing by livestock, and so it is becoming rarer in many areas where it was formerly abundant.

Introduction

Dr. Lewis J. Clark's successful work Wild Flowers of British Columbia *created the demand for these field guides containing most of the large book's colour plates and extending the coverage to include the broader field of the Pacific Northwest. Dr. Clark had completed the first two field guides and had outlined the remaining four prior to his sudden passing. The publishers, with the encouragement of Mrs. Clark, decided to complete the series in his memory with the assistance of Mr. John G. S. Trelawny, B.Sc., Dept. of Biology, University of Victoria.*

It is indeed a very great honour to be asked to continue the work of such a well known personality and prominent botanist as Dr. Lewis Clark, by completing the series of field guides which he was preparing at the time of his death. In this field guide and the one that follows, we have attempted to describe each plant illustrated by Dr. Clark's beautiful coloured photographs as he did with so much feeling in the first two. However, it is difficult to emulate the work of a person so completely absorbed by the wonders of plant life, who had such a uniquely scholarly style of writing; so we have concentrated mainly on producing what we feel is a practical working description of each species within the space available, guided by Dr. Clark's outlines in his outstanding work *Wild Flowers of British Columbia,* and his preparatory notes for this series.

In this field guide we have included most of the common and more colourful wild flowers that may be encountered in the arid regions of the

Pacific Northwest. These regions are shown broadly in the map on the back cover of this handbook. With the exception of eastern Oregon, they cannot be termed 'desert' areas in the true sense of the word; nevertheless they are extremely arid for many months of the year. Moisture-laden air travelling east from the Pacific Ocean precipitates most of its load on the western slopes of the Coast Range and the Cascades; so that the region to the east of these mountains lies in what is known as the 'Rain Shadow'. Here the annual precipitation may be around 20" per year (even as low as 5" in areas of Washington and Oregon). Much of this is in the form of snow in winter, and in summer there may be no more than an occasional thunder shower. A minor Rain Shadow is also evident to the east of Vancouver Island and the Olympic Mountains; so that some of the arid land plants, such as Many-spined Prickly Pear, *Opuntia polyacantha,* may be found on the coastal islands where the summer rainfall is low.

We can look for special features in the plants of these arid regions, adaptations that will enable them to exist successfully in the searing winds and roasting radiance of the sun in summer, as well as in the bitter cold of winter. Their main problem is to obtain and conserve moisture during the long months of summer drought. All green plants must use oxygen, carbon dioxide, and water for their essential metabolic processes of respiration and (in daylight) photosynthesis. They must also give off oxygen and carbon dioxide as waste products, so that their pores (stomata) must remain open for these processes to take place, and this could lead to a serious loss of moisture from inside the plant. However, many plants of the arid lands have adapted to this problem of exchanging gases with the atmosphere with minimal water-loss by the growth of hairs, often very small ones, on their exposed surfaces. These hairy mats serve to trap moist air in pockets, secure from the drying winds, so that loss of moisture from the plant is small. The Common Sagebrush, *Artemisia tridentata* exhibits such hairiness; this species also has small leaves that are readily dropped during extremely dry periods, so that the plant enters a more or less dormant state until enough moisture becomes available to enable it to resume its normal functions. Common Sagebrush has the additional property of possessing roots that can extract the minutest quantities of moisture that may be present in seemingly dry soil; so it is among the most successful plants in the highly competitive struggle for survival in the arid regions; and, where the sparse vegetation is over-grazed, Common Sagebrush will quickly predominate.

Other plants protect themselves from dessication by the presence of a layer of waxy material over their exposed surfaces. This 'cuticle', as it is called, is evident in the fat succulent stems of the cacti such as the Brittle Prickly Pear, *Opuntia fragilis*. Many-spined Prickly Pear, *O. polyacantha* and Cushion Coryphantha, *Coryphantha vivipara*. They have large cells which act as storage tanks for water; thus water-loss is light during the very hot weather, as the plants regulate the opening and the closing of their stomata, so that very little gas exchange with the atmosphere takes place in the daytime. Thus the manufacture of food by photosynthesis is slowed up, which accounts for the very slow rate of growth of the cacti. These plants, as is often painfully discovered, are armed with spiny prickles, that are, in fact, modified leaves. A great many species of plants of the arid regions are protected in this way from grazing by animals, which could otherwise rapidly eliminate whole populations of plants in areas where regeneration is a lengthy and difficult process. Many of our most attractive species of wild flowers, that are not thus protected, are becoming rare as a result of the use of wild land for the grazing of stock.

The beautiful Mariposa Lily, *Calochortus macrocarpus* has become a victim of grazing in some areas. Like all the lilies that have an underground bulb for storage, it relies on being able to accumulate reserves of food that are manufactured in the green leaves during spring and early summer. After flowering and seed-set, the plant withers, and the bulb becomes dormant through the harsh conditions of summer drought and freezing winter, until it comes to life the following spring. To pick the single leafy stalk with its exquisite blooms is to take away its food supply for the following year, so that it will almost certainly die. This would be the end of a living plant that has overcome the hazards of its environment for four years — the time a germinating embryo would probably take until it bore its first indescribably beautiful lavender-coloured flowers, in order that it may reproduce its kind. Let us, then, revel in these marvels of nature and leave them to perpetuate themselves to be enjoyed forever.

We have included, within the scope of this field guide, a description of the type of situation in which each species may be found, giving a very general idea of its habitat.

The range has been given by the approximate north-south, east-west limits. As a rule, no attempt has been made to give individual locations, owing to the dictates of space. 'Our area' (the Pacific Northwest) stretches from Alaska, south through British Columbia, Washington and Oregon to northern California, and east from the coast to the timberline of the Rockies in B.C., the eastern borders of the States of Washington and Oregon, and the northern portion of the California-Nevada boundary.

Dates of flowering are included by stating only the month or months in which flowering may occur. It is meaningless to be any more detailed when we are dealing with such a wide range of altitudes and degrees of latitude in most cases.

The number of introduced species in this field guide is so small that we have discontinued the use of the letters 'I' or 'N' to designate whether a plant is introduced or native, used in Field guides 1 and 2. In the cases of the few introduced species, the fact is mentioned in the text, so further designation is omitted.

We have continued the same general format organized by Dr. Clark in the first two field guides and have stressed the common, or English names, due to some traditional resistance to the exclusive use of scientific names. Concerning the order in which the plants are presented, we have continued to use the same sequence of plant families as that used in the first two field guides, with minor dislocation of this sequence dictated by the necessity of printing vertical and horizontal pictures in pairs.

No keys have been provided, since it has been found on enquiry, that few amateur botanists use them. Further, there is less need for keys in such a small book. Rather it is hoped that the reader will be able, with constant use, to obtain a set of mental images from the pictures, so that recognition in the field will be a comparatively simple procedure.

Scientific terms for various plant structures have been used only where the dictates of space have necessitated brevity. In some cases it has been possible to include a less technical term for explanation in parenthesis. A few of the technical terms used are to be found in the illustrated glossary at the end of the book.

We are greatly indebted for the taxonomy employed to Hitchcock, Cronquist, Ownbey and Thompson in their great 5-volume work *Vascular Plants of the Pacific Northwest;* and to the valuable monographs by Szczawinski and T. M. C. Taylor issued by the Provincial Museum, Victoria. Not included in this series are the trees or ferns (for which several excellent illustrated manuals are available) nor the horsetails, grasses, sedges or rushes (which are of interest chiefly to specialists). However, an effort has been made to include in each book one or more plants that are representative of each of the major families of flowering plants.

We are also more than grateful to the many friends of Dr. Clark who have given so much of their time to offer advice and assistance, and who have lent us slides from their own collections to complete this series. Especially we would like to mention Mrs. J. M. Woollett and Dr. Nancy Turner in this regard, also Mr. Adolf Ceska for his helpful comments on the text, as well as Dr. Marcus Bell and Mr. Stephen Mitchell for the use of the University of Victoria's herbarium facilities.

John Trelawny
Victoria,
British Columbia

2. YELLOW BELL,
Fritillaria pudica
From a small white bulb with tiny rice-like scales, the 6" stems carry two to six smooth, linear leaves and one, rarely two, pendant blossoms about ¾" long. These are at first chromatic yellow, then become more orange with ageing. They appear amongst the sagebrush or in woodland from March to June (according to elevation), from B.C. to n. Cal., e. of Cascades.

3. WASHINGTON LILY,
Lilium washingtonianum
An upright stem 3-6' high, with whorls of lanceolate leaves, rises from a large scaly bulb. Up to 20, or even more, fragrant funnel-form flowers are borne singly on the stem. They are white, turning pink or purple with age and appear from June to Aug. in open forests. Range: Columbia R., s. through Cascades and Sierra Nevada Mts.

4. WOOD LILY,
Lilium philadelphicum

The showy orange flowers are golden-flushed toward the centre and beautifully spotted with maroon-wine. Six tepals, narrow at the base, centre six purple anthers and a three-lobed stigma. The upward-facing blooms, 5" across, are usually solitary at the top of an erect 2' stem, though up to five have been encountered in a single umbel; June-Aug. Narrow leaves are numerous up the stem, the upper ones being in one or two whorls. Found in alkaline meadowland, open woodland and aspen groves. This is the floral emblem for Saskatchewan. In the Pacific Northwest it ranges from s. B.C. s. along the Columbia valley, and eastwards in Wash.

× 0.5

× 1·0

5. NORTHERN BUCKWHEAT, *Eriogonum compositum*
This perennial of dry rocky slopes and cliffs has a strong woody tap-root which supports a more or less prostrate branched stem. Leaves, on long slender stalks, are ovate to heart-shaped. They are green above, white-woolly beneath, and persistent after withering; the whole forming mat-like clumps up to 1' wide. Quarter-inch creamy-white to deep lemon-yellow flowers are borne in compound umbels on leafless stalks about 1' tall, in May and June. Range: e. side of Cascades from Wash. to n. Cal., e. to n.e. Ore.

× 1·0

6. DOUGLAS' BUCKWHEAT, *Eriogonum douglasii*
Dense-matted and shrubby, this species is rarely over 4" high. Typically the flowering-stems bear a whorl of leaves near the middle. These and the basal leaves are woolly on the lower side, sometimes on the upper surface also; generally they are linear, the basal ones about ¾" long, those on the stem smaller. Flowers in tight round umbels are white or lemon-yellow to pinkish; May-July. Found in Sagebrush flats and dry open hillsides, or among Ponderosa Pines. Range: e. of Cascades from c. Wash. to n.e. Cal.

7   × 0·2

8   × 0·1

7. YELLOW BUCKWHEAT, *Eriogonum flavum*
An extremely variable species, with flowering-stems rising 4-12″ above a mat of grey leaves. Typically the leaves are at least ¼″ long, paddle-shaped and densely white-haired, particularly beneath. The yellow flowers, in bloom from early July to early Sept. are rank-smelling. Common in open arid regions. Range: s.e. B.C., extreme e. Wash. to n.e. Ore.

8. PUSSY-PAWS, *Spraguea umbellata*
The much-branched prostrate stem forms a dense mat of leathery spatulate leaves up to 6″ broad. Four-inch reddish stalks bear rounded heads of white to pinkish flowers that bloom from early June to Aug. Found amongst Ponderosa Pine and in open subalpine dry places. Range: s. B.C. to n. Cal., mostly e. of Cascades.

9　× 0·4

9. SULPHUR FLOWER, *Eriogonum umbellatum*
An extremely variable species in which forms can be found from 4-12″ high. Flower-stems have leaves which may vary from narrow to broad, usually greyish-hairy beneath and smooth-greenish above. These are all basal except for a whorl immediately beneath the umbel. The flowers, in clusters, vary from pale to deep yellow or cream, often becoming flecked with rose as they age; June-Aug. Found in dry Sagebrush habitats and up to considerable elevations. Range: s. B.C. to n.e. Cal. mostly e. of Cascades.

10 HABITAT

11   × 0.5

10. RED GLASSWORT, *Salicornia rubra*
This bright red glasswort decorates the borders of alkaline lakes and sloughs and areas of salty soil. The minute flowers are in groups of 3, sunk in depressions at the joints of the fleshy spikes, the central flowers being above the two lateral ones; June to Sept. Range: s. Dry Interior B.C., and e. Wash.

11. BABY'S BREATH, *Gypsophila paniculata*
This Eurasian member of the pink family has escaped from cultivation, and has become established in rather dry places in s. B.C. and e. Wash. From thick perennial roots spring freely-branched stems up to 4' tall, with numerous lanceolate leaves. Compound cymes (branched inflorescences) bear a profusion of tiny white flowers; June-Aug.

13 × 0.4

12 × 1.0

12. TUMBLEWEED,
Salsola kali
The many-branched stems may grow to 4', forming an almost globular bushy plant. The leaves are alternate, ½-2" long, and tipped with a sharp point. Tiny green flowers at the base of each leaf produce one seed each during the summer months. This Eurasian weed was imported into S. Dakota in 1877, and it has spread through the arid regions of S. B.C to n.e. Cal., mostly e. of Cascades.

13. WHITE VIRGIN'S BOWER,
Clematis ligusticifolia
This common woody vine is found along creek bottoms in Sagebrush and Ponderosa Pine country. The pinnate leaves usually have 5 ovate leaflets. Abundant small creamy-white blooms are borne in clusters on short stems arising from the leaf-axils, male and female flowers being separate; May-Aug. Range: s. B.C. and Wash. e. of Cascades, both sides of Cascades, Ore. to n. Cal. (Introduced on Vancouver Island.)

14. BITTER ROOT,
Lewisia rediviva

This is a remarkable plant of open, dry, rocky slopes and sagebrush plains. It has relatively large, forked, fat rhizomes that, after the first rains of waning summer, sprout a thick tuft of succulent leaves resembling large plump fir needles. These leaves survive the winter, but begin to shrivel, and are often quite withered away by the following May when the brilliant white, pink, or rose blossoms appear. Each 2" flower (with its 12-18 petals) is solitary, carried about 3" above the ground, and ripens 6-20 shiny brown seeds. Range: s. B.C., Wash. and Ore., e. of Cascades to n. Cal.

15. TWEEDY'S LEWISIA,
Lewisia tweedyi

This truly beautiful plant can be found growing in crevices on rocky slopes among Ponderosa Pine in the Wenatchee Mts., Wash. The thick fleshy tap-root gives rise to a cluster of broadly ovate leaves, with broad petioles the same length as the leaf-blades. Several 6-8" flower-stems each bear 1-5 striking flowers. These have 8 or 9 petals, about 1½" long, varying from delicate shades of salmon pink to pale yellow; May-July.

Mrs. J. Woollett

16 × 0·2

17 × 1·3

16. BLUE CLEMATIS, *Clematis columbiana*
Nowhere abundant, this rather delicate vine is found in open woods and on talus slopes e. of Cascades, from B.C. s. through Wash. to n.e. Ore. Opposite leaves are 3-foliate, the leaflets pointed-ovate. Petals are lacking; the 4 showy blue to purple sepals take their place. These are followed by a fragile mop of plume-tailed achenes (dried fruit); May-July.

17. SAGEBRUSH BUTTERCUP, *Ranunculus glaberrimus*
This perennial is seldom more than 5 to 6" tall, and bears a number of showy, bright yellow, waxy blooms 1-1½" wide with broad petals. Smooth leaves are chiefly basal, blunt spoon-shaped, and usually entire, except for 2 notches at the tip. Widespread through Sagebrush and Ponderosa Pine country. Range: s. B.C. through Wash. and Ore. to n. Cal., e. of Cascades.

18. GOLDEN CORYDALIS, *Corydalis aurea*

A sprawling much-branched plant up to 18" long, with many handsome blue-green, thrice pinnately-divided leaves which far exceed the short racemes (flower-spikes) in length. Brilliant golden 1½"-long blooms, having an upper petal that is characteristically hooded, give way to 1"-long capsules bearing shiny black seeds; May-July. Found in moist to well-drained open places e. of Coast Range in Alas. and B.C., e. of Cascades Wash., s. to n. Cal.

19. ROUND-LEAVED ALUMROOT, *Heuchera cylindrica*

This highly variable species bears small cream to greenish-yellow bell-shaped flowers on 6" to 2' stalks; Apr.-Aug. Long-petioled basal leaves vary considerably in shape, number of lobes, and degree of hairiness; but generally they are longer than broad. Inhabits rocky soil and talus. Range: in Cascades and e., s. and c. Interior B.C., to n. Cal.

20. FLIXWEED,
Descurainia sophia

A member of the mustard family is this introduced weed from Europe. The 1-3', occasionally-branched, stem bears many pinnately-compound leaves on the lower half. Tiny greenish-yellow flowers at the tip of the spike are followed by erect 1" siliques (seed-pods): Mar.-July. Widespread in waste places and roadside ditches throughout the Pacific N.W.

21. TUMBLEMUSTARD,
Sisymbrium altissimum

A coarse, introduced European weed, this freely-branched annual, up to 5' tall, has leaves that are up to 6" long and deeply cleft, with narrow segments. Tiny pale-yellow flowers in terminal clusters bloom May-Sept., giving way to siliques (seed-pods) that reach 4" in length. Widespread in waste places throughout our range.

22. YELLOW SPIDERFLOWER, *Cleome lutea*
Stems up to 3' high are topped with showy clusters of bright yellow flowers, each with 6 long hair-like stamens suggestive of spiders' legs. These are followed by 1½" rather drooping seed-pods. The leaves are smooth and palmately-compound, each with 4-5 lanceolate leaflets. This attractive annual decorates areas of sandy or rocky soil in open desert from May to July, ranging from e. Wash. to n.e. Cal.

23. COMMON SAXIFRAGE,
Saxifraga bronchialis

This beautiful perennial rock cover has evergreen leaves that are sufficiently variable to result in plants that appear quite unlike. They vary from harsh, slim-lanceolate and sharp-tipped, with rigid stubby cilia along the margins, to plants with much softer, thumb-shaped leaves with smaller, softer hairs. From June to Aug., 2-6", much branched, flowering-stems rise from the dense mat of leaves. Each branch is terminated by a round bud or a showy ½" flower. The oval, white to cream petals are dotted with a series of round spots of pure spectrum tints, graduated from tip to base in crimson, through orange to chrome-yellow. Found from sea-level rocks to high alpine screes and open slopes, Alas. to n. Ore.

24 × 1·0

24. SQUAW CURRANT, *Ribes cereum*
A common unarmed shrub of the eastern slopes of the Cascades from B.C. to n. Cal., found on Sagebrush flats to subalpine regions. Up to 6′ tall, it has small, scarcely-lobed, roundish leaves, rather wider than long, that are grey-green, and often minutely hairy on both surfaces. Whitish to pinkish, drooping, urn-shaped flowers appear from April to June, followed by dull to bright red unpalatable fruit.

25   × 0.5

26   × 0.4

25. STICKY CURRANT, *Ribes viscosissimum*
A straggly thornless shrub, up to 6′ tall, that is covered with downy hairs secreting a sticky gum. The 5-lobed leaves are 1½-3″ broad. Small tubular flowers, grouped 6-12 in semi-erect, rounded clusters, are greenish, sometimes purplish-tinged; May-June. They are followed by blue-black unpalatable berries. Found in dry to moist habitats to timberline, on open to wooded slopes. Range: B.C. to n. Cal., and e. to Rockies.

26. PURPLE AVENS, *Geum triflorum*
Reddish, 1′-high flowering-stems bear 3 nodding, bell-shaped flowers that are dull purple or pinkish (April-early Aug.). The seeds are attractively adorned with long-tailed, feathery plumes. Leaves are hairy and finely-dissected. Found in moister parts of the Sagebrush country to subalpine levels. Range: Cascades, B.C. to n. Cal., and eastwards.

27 × 0·6

28 × 0·5

27. SHRUBBY CINQUEFOIL, *Potentilla fruticosa*
A showy deciduous plant that forms a rounded bush 2-4' high, a unique feature in the cinquefoils. Leaves are small and greyish-green, with a short hairy petiole and 3-5 untoothed leaflets. The flowers are intensely yellow, especially at higher levels, and the seeds bear a short tuft of hairs; late June-Aug. Common on dry plains and subalpine slopes throughout the Pacific Northwest.

28. CHOKE CHERRY, *Prunus virginiana*
Tall shrubs up to 20', with smooth reddish-brown bark. The leaves are more sharply pointed than those of its near relative the Bitter Cherry, and the numerous flowers are carried in long racemes (spikes) rather than rounded clusters; May-early July. The ripe fruit, astringent to taste, is bluish-purple. Found in moist places in Sagebrush desert or grasslands. Range: s. B.C. to n. Cal., generally e. of Coast Range.

29. STICKY CINQUEFOIL,
Potentilla glandulosa
A very common and variable species in moist places in open woodland or grasslands, s.w. B.C. to n. Cal., and e. to Rockies. The leaves are pinnate, with 5-9 leaflets; the stems (up to 2' high, often a reddish colour and hairy) bear pale yellow to cream-coloured flowers, each with 25-40 stamens, from late May to early July.

30. GREASEWOOD,
Purshia tridentata
This is a rigid shrub 3-9' tall, with inconspicuous flowers whose small yellow petals quickly drop. Each flower is carried stiffly alone at the end of an abbreviated short shoot; Apr.-June. The leaves roll inward in scorching weather, exposing the greyish, densely hairy underside. This is a desert shrub found in sagebrush or Ponderosa Pine country. Range: s. B.C. to n. Cal., e. of Cascades.

31. WOOD'S ROSE,
Rosa woodsii
This is a highly variable species whose stems, armed with slender, straight prickles do not usually exceed 3' in height. Flowers (1½" in diameter) have smooth sepals (May-July); and the 5-9, often crowded, leaflets sometimes are rather coarsely-toothed. Dry plains. Range: s.e. B.C., to n. Cal., e. of Cascades.

32. PYRAMID SPIRAEA,
Spiraea pyramidata
This usually erect shrub, up to 4' tall, is topped by 4" long, foamy, cone-shaped clusters of palest pink or nearly white flowers; June-Aug. Found in valleys (often near water), to dry slopes. Range: central B.C. to n. Ore., e. of Cascades.

33 × 0·5

33. WEEDY MILK VETCH, *Astragalus miser*
A widespread and extremely variable species of legume that is distinctive in its very narrow leaflets and in its flower colouring. Flowers are white, sometimes light pinkish-purple, the keel usually purplish-tipped, and the banner and wings bluish-pencilled; May-June. The flowers are followed by stalkless, drooping, lightly hairy, 1″ pods. Common in grasslands and foothills to above timber line in rather moist to open dry places. Range: s. B.C. and n. Wash., e. of Cascades.

34. SILKY LUPINE,
Lupinus sericeus

This highly variable perennial is common in Sagebrush and Ponderosa Pine regions. From a branching crown rise one to several erect stems 12-24" tall. Leaves are numerous, each with 5-9 leaflets up to 2" in length. Long white silky hairs cover both leaves and stem. Crowded spikes of deep-blue flowers bloom May-Aug. Range: e. of Cascades, B.C. s. to n. Cal., e. to Rockies.

35. SANDFAIN,
Onobrychis viciaefolia

This perennial legume (a European feed plant for livestock) has become established in some areas of B.C. and Wash. The pinnately-compound leaves may have up to 27 elliptical leaflets. Tightly packed flower-spikes can have as many as 50 showy pink-to-lavender flowers, each corolla lined with brilliant purple stripes (June-Aug.).

× 0.5

36. YELLOW LOMENTS, *Hedysarum sulphurescens*
This perennial develops, from a thick woody tap-root, a cluster of 12-24 inch stems, bearing pinnate leaves, and rather one-sided spikes of drooping, pale, yellowish-white, pea-type flowers; June to Aug. The plant is at once identifiable when the fruits develop. They are long, flattened pendulous pods (loments), remarkably constricted between each of the 2-4 seeds. Found in open wooded areas. Range: e. slope of Cascades, B.C.s. to Okanagan Co. Wash., e. to Rockies.

37. LATE YELLOW LOCOWEED,
Oxytropis campestris

These plants are much-branched from the base, 9-18" tall, with 11-31 lanceolate leaflets, densely silky-haired on both surfaces. A highly variable species, flowers are white to yellowish, sometimes with a purple keel; May-July. Found in rather dry areas in montane to submontane regions. Range: Alas., s. through central B.C., in Olympics, Wash., eastwards across Rockies.

38. PINK FAIRIES,
Clarkia pulchella

A most beautiful annual, not more than 1½' tall, with thin linear leaves. Striking flowers have 4 petals that are glowing pink and deeply-notched into 3 lobes; May-June. Common in open, dry grassy or Sagebrush areas. Range: Columbia R. valley, s. B.C., southward e. of Cascades to s.e. Ore., e. to Rockies.

39. SHOWY OXYTROPIS, *Oxytropis splendens*
Beautiful silky compound leaves form a dense basal cluster 6-10" high. Their very numerous leaflets are arranged in whorls of 3 to 6. They are pointed-elliptical, from ¼" to 1" long. The flower-stalks generally lengthen to hold the dense purple spike slightly above the mass of silvery foliage. Flowers, opening June-Aug., are about ½" long, with a densely white-haired calyx about half as long. The beak of the keel is slender and straight (or slightly curved), and the pod is slim-pointed, about ½" long. Found in meadowland on the lower slopes of the Rockies (mostly on the e. side), from Alas. s.

40. BIG-HEADED CLOVER, *Trifolium macrocephalum*

Large showy 2"-wide flower-heads distinguish this from the other clovers. They are solitary and terminal on stems about 6" tall. From April to June the attractive flowers (white through palest salmon to rose pink) appear, each with a calyx of characteristic long plume-like teeth. Five to nine leaflets of the palmately-compound leaves are leathery and sometimes almost heart-shaped. Found in Sagebrush and Ponderosa Pine regions. Range: central Wash., s. to e. Ore.

41. WILD BLUE FLAX,
Linum perenne

There are two distinct varieties of blue flax: one is native to N. America, its flowers are all alike. The other variety, a cultivated plant from Eurasia, has become established occasionally in waste places in the Pacific Northwest. This one has two types of flowers, one with styles longer than the stamens, the other vice versa. The species is perennial, about 2' tall, with alternate, narrow, linear leaves that are 1" long. Flowers in open spikes have 5 bright sky-blue petals, June-Aug., from sea level to alpine regions. Wild Blue Flax may be found in dry, open places. Range: Alas. e. of Coast Range, e. of Cascades from B.C. to n. Cal.

42 × 0·9

42. STICKY GERANIUM, *Geranium viscosissimum*

This beautiful species is common in the dry lands east of the Cascades from B.C. to n. Cal. Strong branching stems, from 10-30" tall, bear deeply-lobed leaves, that may be 4" across. Flowers are freely produced and handsome, being as much as 1½" wide and bright rosy-pink; May-Aug. The sepals are glandular-haired, and bristle-tipped. Petals bear short hairs near their bases, and are somewhat wavy-edged. Not infrequently white (and occasionally deep purple) individuals are seen. The fruit, typical of this family, is beaked — ½" long (including the stigmas). Stem, leaves, and flower-stalks are covered with sticky hairs.

43   × 0·5

43. POISON IVY, *Rhus radicans*
The shiny leaves have 3 leaflets. They are pointed with a rounded base and wavy edges, smooth above and usually hairy beneath. Numerous greenish-white flowers, in erect clusters, are borne on short stalks — either terminal, or arising from the axils of the leaves from April to July. They are succeeded by smooth, whitish fruits (drupes) about ¼" in diameter. In the dry Sagebrush plains of the Interior, Poison Ivy is generally erect, up to 4-5' high; but nearer the Coast, its habit is somewhat trailing, among grasses. A toxic oil in all parts of the plant causes severe skin irritation after contact. Range: Dry Interior s. B.C., s. through Wash. and Ore., e. of Cascades.

44 × 0·1

45 × 0·4

44. SUMAC, *Rhus glabra*
The bare branches of this unmistakable shrub have, by April, become conspicuous with large, dark-purplish, tightly packed cones of flower-buds. These produce tiny greenish-yellow flowers, April-July, which are succeeded in the fall by reddish, densely-hairy fruits. By October the large leaves, each with 7-29 pointed-elliptical leaflets, have turned an incandescent scarlet or flaming yellow. Adorns dry open forested regions at lower levels. Range: Dry Interior of B.C., Wash., Ore., and n. Cal. e. of Cascades.

45. SNOWBRUSH, *Ceanothus velutinus*
This strong-scented, evergreen shrub, up to 6′ tall, has leathery, sticky-varnished leaves, with three prominent main veins. Dense clusters of small, greenish-white flowers cover the bushes from June to Aug. Found in dry, rather open places. Range: Dry Interior of B.C., Wash. to n. Cal., e. of Cascades on lower slopes. Occasionally found on Vancouver I., Gulf Islands, and lower slopes of Olympics.

47. BRITTLE PRICKLY PEAR.
Opuntia fragilis

This savagely-armed plant spreads its mats of fleshy jointed stems over the parched hillsides of the drylands from B.C. s., chiefly e., of Cascades, to n. Cal. Brittle Prickly Pear can be distinguished from its companion species, **48**, whose range it overlaps, even though they are very alike. The cluster of pads is lower than those of **48**, and the joints are almost round in cross-section, never greatly flattened. The long spines are generally fewer in each cluster in this species, and the filaments are most often reddish in the huge flowers, which are pale to deep yellow, almost never ageing to reddish, as do those of **48**. Both species are found along the rocky shore-line in the Gulf Islands; but Brittle Prickly Pear appears to be the more common on S. Vancouver I. and the neighbouring islands.

46. CUSHION CORYPHANTHA, *Coryphantha vivipara*

This cactus is found mainly east of the Rockies, and it appears within our range only in the desert valleys and hills of s.e. Oregon. The globose stems, about 2½" tall and the same width, are pointed at the base. The surface is made up of rounded projections, each with a rosette of spines of two sizes, the longer being about ½". One inch-long flowers are a bright reddish-purple, and are followed by a greenish fruit; May-June.

49   × 0.4

50   × 0.4

49. BLAZING STAR, *Mentzelia laevicaulis*
This is a biennial (or short-lived perennial) up to 3′ tall, that bears 3-4″ bright golden star-like flowers, July to Sept. These have 5 long, sharply-pointed sepals, and 5 pointed petals interspaced with 5 smaller petals. The 2-3″ oblong leaves are lobed like a dandelion. Found in wastelands and roadsides in desert areas. Range: central, s. and s.e. B.C., e. Wash., s. to n.e. Cal.

50. SILVER-BERRY, *Elaeagnus commutata*
A very distinctive shrub up to 12′ high, with striking 1-3″ long pointed-oval leaves. From the leaf-axils, almost stemless flowers appear in twos and threes in June and July. These consist of a 4-lobed tubular calyx, silvered without, yellow within, and they are highly aromatic. Found on dry gravel benches and in gullies. Range: Alas. s. to Dry Interior B.C., e. to Rockies.

48. MANY-SPINED PRICKLY PEAR,
Opuntia polyacantha

In this species of cactus the yellow flowers are often tinged with apricot, and may fade almost reddish; the filaments are usually yellow. Joints of the stem are strongly flattened, and tenacious, so that even the terminal segment is not readily detached. On these segments numerous long spines radiate from raised pores (areoles), more per areole than in **47**. In May and June, the Prickly Pear enlivens the drab flatlands with its quite amazing flowers. Though this remarkable plant occurs in the Gulf Islands, s. Vancouver I., and n.e. coast of the Olympic Peninsula, it seldom develops numerous flowers until the plant encounters the dry hot air of the arid Interior, where it ranges from B.C. s. to e. Ore., e. to Rockies.

51. EVENING PRIMROSE, *Oenothera biennis*

This species is an erect biennial, with leafy stems 2-4' tall. The plant is greyish, with short hairs; but some longer hairs on the lower stem and beneath the flower clusters are unusual, because they have a reddish swollen base. Leaves are lanceolate, 2-7" long, entire to slightly-toothed. The delicately fragrant flowers spread their softly radiant, primrose saucers as evening falls. From June to Sept., the flowers open nightly — a few at a time — from a crowded terminal bud-cluster. The broad overlapping petals are thin and delicate, up to 1" long. They generally age pinkish-orange to purplish. Found in meadowland and along stream banks from the plains to the lower mountains, throughout the Pacific N.W.

52   × 0.4

53   × 0.2   Dr. N. Turner

52. PINK OENOTHERA, *Oenothera pallida*
This is a perennial, woody, much-branched plant up to 20" tall. Stems are sometimes smooth, but more often greyish-haired. The numerous lanceolate leaves are 1-2" long, with entire to sometimes deeply-toothed margins. Delicate flowers open white, the petals quickly becoming pink-edged, and soon age to soft purplish-pink. Found on sandy or gravelly soil in arid open places. Range: dry areas of s. B.C., e. Wash., and e. Ore.

53. LARGE-FRUITED LOMATIUM, *Lomatium macrocarpum*
A thick tap-root gives rise to a crown of bushy thrice-compound pinnate leaves. Out of this arise stalks bearing umbels of small white flowers, occasionally tinged yellowish or purplish. A common, highly variable species in dry open plains and rocky places e. of Cascades, from B.C. to n. Cal.

54 × 0·5

54. WESTERN AZALEA, *Rhododendron occidentale*
This spreading shrub, up to 15' tall, is among the finest cultivated species of Azalea. It grows wild in one area only: in the moist wooded regions from the Umpqua River, Ore., s. to n. Cal., in the coast ranges and in the Sierra Nevada. The deciduous leaves are thin, bright yellow and up to 3½" long. Flowers, 5-20 in terminal clusters, May-July, have an attractive scent. Lobes of the corolla are white to deep pink, the lower lobe having a deep yellowish blotch.

55   × 0.4

56   × 0.9

55. SHOWY MILKWEED, *Asclepias speciosa*
This striking plant, 2-4' tall, has opposite, 2½-5" long, leathery leaves. Clusters of round buds open to reveal pink flowers. Each one is a complicated structure with 5 pink petals and 5 curved horns protruding from a stamen-tube; June-Aug. The stems exude a sticky latex when broken. Found in dry to moist soil. Range: s. B.C. to n. Cal., e. side of Cascades.

56. FIELD BINDWEED, *Convolvulus arvensis*
An introduced persistent weed from Europe, Field Bindweed has become well established in many areas throughout the Pacific N.W., with its deep wide-running rootstocks. The trailing stems, usually 6-8", can be 6' long in rich soil. Leaves alternate on the stem, bearing flower-stalks at their axils. The flowers have a deeply 5-lobed calyx-cup, and a white or pink bell-shaped corolla with 5 pronounced ribs.

57. SCARLET GILIA, *Gilia aggregata*
This is a truly spectacular plant. The numerous tubular flowers with flared corolla-tubes are a vivid red, startling in intensity, marked with small white spots; May-Aug. In subalpine broken rock the plant may be 4″ tall, compact above the basal rosette of carrot-like foliage; but in open woods with rich soil, the much-branched sparse-leaved stems may reach 3′. Range: s. B.C. to n. Cal., e. of Cascades.

58   × 0·5

59   × 1·1

58. SPINY PHLOX, *Leptodactylon pungens*
Buds, usually flushed with lavender, are followed by typically phlox-like white flowers that open during the night, May-July. These and the foliage are sweetly aromatic. Thin needle-like leaves are clustered on the branchlets, and they are grey and persistent at the branch bases when dead. This rather dense shrub 4-24" tall, is an attractive feature of severely arid areas e. of Cascades from s. B.C. to n. Cal.

59. TUFTED PHLOX, *Phlox caespitosa*
A tap-rooted, dwarf, tufted phlox, up to 6" tall, rather similar to **58,** but much smaller. Leaves up to ½" long are very narrow, and the white, pink, or mauve flowers are solitary on the ends of the branches; Apr.-June. Found in open or partly-shaded places amongst Ponderosa Pines. Range: s. B.C., c. Wash., n.e. Ore.

60. PERIWINKLE PHLOX,
Phlox adsurgens

This attractive little perennial has several upward curving stems to 1' high, with paired opposite pointed-elliptical leaves. Each pale pink flower has a ¾"-long corolla-tube that widens into 5- ½"-long lobes, the stamens staggered within the tube. The flowers are borne in cymes (open inflorescences) from May to August. Found on wooded slopes up to moderate elevations. Range: n.w. Cal. and s.w. Ore., w. side of Cascades.

61. LONG-LEAVED PHLOX,
Phlox longifolia

This pink or white Phlox, with sweetly-scented flowers, has upright stems up to 20", though 8-10" is more usual. The smooth 3"-long leaves are opposite up the stem. Characteristically stiff vertical ridges line the calyx-tube. Flowers may be as much as 1¼" wide; April-July. Found in dry plains and open rocky slopes up to considerable elevations. Range: s. B.C., to n. Cal., e. of Cascades.

62. COMMON ANCHUSA,
Anchusa officinalis

A common cultivated species, native to Europe, that has escaped and become established in areas mostly e. of Cascades, s. B.C. to Ore., also s. Vancouver I. This is a deep taprooted perennial, up to 30" tall, hairy all over, and with showy deep blue flowers. These are borne in curled terminal spikes on many branches; May-July.

63   × 1·0

64   × 2·0

63. FIDDLE-NECK, *Amsinckia intermedia*
This is a weed of disturbed ground (roadsides and waste places), from B.C. to n. Cal. It is covered in bristly hairs, and may be 30″ tall; aptly named from the arrangement of the flowers in coiled, fiddle-scroll spikes. The corolla-tube is orange-yellow; Apr.-May.

64. VARIED-LEAVED PHACELIA, *Phacelia heterophylla*
The usually single, erect stems (up to 4′) bear greyish-green prominently veined leaves. The lower ones are conspicuously lobed, becoming entire upwards. The whole plant is covered in fine hairs, with long bristles on the stem and inflorescence. Flowers, dullish-white, rarely purplish, are borne in tight clusters; May to July. A widespread species of dry places in the plains and foothills from s. B.C. to n. Cal., more common e. of Cascades.

65 × 1·5

65. NARROW-LEAVED PHACELIA, *Phacelia linearis*

This widespread showy annual has a single stem 4-20″ high, branched above, and sometimes bearing crowded groups of flowers in the axils of all the upper leaves. Stem, leaves, and calyx are densely fine-haired. Leaves are alternate, at first simple and linear, but developing side-lobes upward. Broadly bell-shaped, the corolla may span ¾″, and vary in colour from white through pale lavender to bluish-violet. Common from June-Aug. in alkaline flats and arid open plains and foothills. Range: s. B.C. to n. Cal., mostly e. of Cascades.

66. DWARF HESPEROCHIRON,
Hesperochiron pumilus

This tiny plant, not more than 2" high, grows in open meadows from the plains to moderate elevations from Wash. to n. Cal., e. of the Cascade summits. Two or three fascinating little white flowers, centred yellow with pencilled lines on the petals, bloom from April to June. They are supported on single stalks that, like the smooth ovate leaves, rise from a stem-like tap-root. Another similar but more robust species, CALIFORNIA HESPEROCHIRON, *Hesperochiron californicus*, prefers more alkaline situations. Its range includes that of the dwarf species, but extends much further south, out of our range.

67. COMMON HOUND'S TONGUE,
Cynoglossum officinale
This is a weedy biennial immigrant from Europe, strongly established along roadsides throughout the Pacific Northwest, from B.C. southward. It is a coarse plant, up to 4' tall, with dull reddish-purple flowers (May-July), followed by 4-clustered burs that readily catch on clothing and hair.

68. GROMWELL,
Lithospermum ruderale
A coarse perennial with several leafy stems growing 10-20" from a large woody tap-root. Many linear, closely clustered leaves clasp the stem, which like the lower leaf-surfaces is covered in long white hairs. The greenish-yellow flowers, almost hidden in the leaf-axils, are pleasantly fragrant; April-June. Found in open dry places in valleys and up to moderate elevations. Range: s. B.C. to n. Cal., mostly e. of Cascades, also in Puget Sound area.

69. LEAFY LUNGWORT,
Mertensia oblongifolia

Also called 'Bluebells' (not to be confused with the Scottish 'Bluebells'; *Campanula rotundifolia*), this is an attractive flower on the lower level Ponderosa Pine-Sagebrush flats and foothills of s.e. B.C., and Wash. e. of Cascades. A spring flower, the pink buds open into attractive blue long-tubed 'bells' in April and May. (Very similar to another species — LUNGWORT, *M. longiflora* — of almost the same range, though extending s. to Ore.) The one illustrated has a cluster of basal leaves as well as stem leaves, and the leaves are more pointed. The flower-stems are in clumps rather than solitary, and the floral-tube is shorter, and lobes are more flared than in the latter.

70. PALLID PAINTBRUSH,
Castilleja sulphurea
Like all the 'Paintbrushes' this is a perennial plant that is parasitic on the roots of others. The clustered stems may be 20" tall with many alternate linear leaves. Coloured bracts that enclose the flowers are pale yellow or cream-coloured. A long hooked projection of the floral-tube (galea) extends beyond these bracts. Found in moist open places up to high elevations in the Rockies (s.e. B.C.).

71. COMMON MULLEIN,
Verbascum thapsus
This introduced European biennial is now widespread in dry places, mostly e. of Cascades, from B.C. to n. Cal., and sporadic in s. Vancouver I. and the Gulf Islands. Tall, densely-furred sentinel stalks rise 5 or 6' from a first-year rosette of great flannel leaves. From June onwards, through the summer months, small pleasant-smelling yellow flowers open erratically up and down the tall flowering-spike.

71 × 0·2

70 × 0·4

72   × 0·8

72. SHRUBBY PENSTEMON, *Penstemon fruticosus*
This is a variable species, beautiful in all its forms. These perennial plants are semi-evergreen, a proportion of the leaves usually turning reddish in the fall, and later dropping. Commonly the compact framework of branches is 6-12″ tall. Leaves are generally without hairs, up to 2″ long, but usually shorter, elliptical, and entire, but in var. *scouleri* (illustrated here) they are much narrower and obscurely toothed. Flowers up to 2″ long are generally blue-lavender, but vary to white or pink; May-Aug. Found in rocky open or wooded places from foothills to 1000 ft. Range: s. B.C. to c. Ore., e. of Cascades.

73. GAIRDNER'S PENSTEMON,
Penstemon gairdneri
This bushy little perennial, up to 16″ tall, has many erect flowering-stems as well as short leafy sterile stems forming a loose mat, the leaves entire and linear. Tubular flowers, lavender to bright rose-purple, are ¾″ long; May-June. Found in dry, open, rocky places, (sometimes with Sagebrush), from plains to moderate elevations. Range: e. of Cascades in Wash. and Ore.

74 × 2·2

74. RYDBERG'S PENSTEMON, *Penstemon rydbergii*
This showy plant of moist grassy slopes in foothills is also found in drier Sagebrush areas. Flower stems, up to 28″ tall, rise from rosettes of oblanceolate basal leaves. Stem leaves are opposite and stalkless; all are smooth. A whorl of horizontal tubular, bluish-purple flowers crowns the stem from late May to July. Range: s. Wash. to n. Cal., mostly e. of Cascades.

75. INDIAN WHEAT,
Plantago purshii
A small silky-pubescent annual (up to 5″) of open dry plains and foothills from s. B.C. to n. Cal., e. of Cascades. The flower-spikes are crowded with tiny chaffy flowers appearing generally in May and June. This member of the Plantain family has the synonym *P. patagonica*, being also found in Argentina and Chile.

76. PINK PUSSY-TOES,
Antennaria rosea
Very similar to **94**, though found at lower elevations. This species has distinctive rosy bracts, ageing whitish, and occasionally never developing the typical pink colour. The bracts are blunt-pointed, not round-tipped as in **94**. Blooms May to Aug., in dry open places and open woods from plains to moderate elevations. Range: Alas. to n. Cal., e. of Cascades from s. B.C. to n. Cal.

77. PALE AGOSERIS, *Agoseris glauca*

Sometimes called 'Fall Dandelion' or 'False Dandelion', this is an extremely variable plant. It has a basal clump of narrow lanceolate greyish leaves up to 12" long, widely-toothed or with entire margins. The handsome yellow 'composite' flowers on single stalks dry to pinkish, and are followed by ½"-long achenes. Blooms May to Sept., according to locality. Found in open dry places from s. Alas. southward, sporadic in s.w. B.C. and w. Wash., generally e. of Cascades from s. B.C. to n. Cal.

78. LESSER BURDOCK,
Arctium minus

A widespread coarse weed from Eurasia, this plant can reach 4½' in height. Very large triangular leaves may be 24" long. The rough involucre has a dense coat of black hooked bracts enclosing heads of purplish flowers; July-Oct. Established in roadsides and waste places throughout our range. A larger species, GREAT BURDOCK, *A. lappa*, is more common in the Dry Interior.

79. SHINING ARNICA,
Arnica fulgens

A densely grey-pubescent perennial with stems up to 1' high, having opposite leaves. These and the basal ones are narrow, with entire margins. Usually solitary flowers are bright yellowish-orange; May-July. Found in open grassy places in foothills and at moderate elevations. Range: s. B.C. to n. Cal., e. of Cascades.

80. PASTURE WORMWOOD,
Artemisia frigida

Also called 'Pasture Sage' this is a diminutive, silvered, subshrub with a pleasant sage fragrance. The much-split, almost hair-like, leaves are densely white-haired on both surfaces. Flower-heads are pale yellow, and clustered towards the ends of the semi-erect branchlets; July-Sept. Found on dry open slopes, from the plains to about 3000'. Range: n. Alas., s. through interior B.C., e. to Rockies.

81. COMMON SAGEBRUSH,
Artemisia tridentata

The gnarled, grey-green, 2-5' branches of Sagebrush, with their shredded bark and wedge-shaped, 3-notched, grey leaves are a familiar sight in arid plains to moderate elevations in the mountains. Tiny flower-heads contain 3-5 (up to 8 in higher altitude forms) brownish-yellow, rather drab flowers, blooming Sept. Range: Dry Interior B.C. to n. Cal., Cascades eastwards.

82. HOOKER'S BALSAM-ROOT, *Balsamorhiza hookeri*

Unlike **83**, the leaves of this species are deeply-segmented. They appear in basal tufts from a carrot-like tap-root. Leafless stems, about 1' tall, bear solitary, 2"-wide, golden flower-heads; April-June. Found in dry rocky places in the plains and foothills of central Wash.

83   × 0·2

84   × 0·4

83. ARROW-LEAF BALSAM-ROOT, *Balsamorhiza sagittata*
Large, greyish-green, 'arrowhead' leaves, 6" wide and 12" long, with even longer petioles, form impressive tufts on open hillsides, up to moderate elevations in the mountains. Flower-stems, 10-30" tall, each bear a single bright yellow showy head that may be 4" across; April-July. This plant is grazed by stock; and shoots, roots, and seeds were included in the diet of the Interior tribes. Range: s. B.C. to n. Cal., from w. slopes of Cascades eastward.

84. GOLDEN ASTER, *Chrysopis villosa*
A variable perennial, sometimes erect and 20" tall, but more often sprawling and 4-5" high. Soft-haired leaves appear greyish-green, and they are alternate, entire and strap-shaped. From June to Sept., bright yellow flower-heads appear. These are about 1" across, consisting of a ring of 10-25 pistillate ray-florets, enclosing many tube-florets that have both stamens and pistils. Occurs in open sandy soil from s. B.C. to n. Cal.

85. TUFTED WHITE PRAIRIE ASTER,
Aster pansies

A tall perennial, up to 6' high, bearing numerous small white-rayed flower heads; June-Sept. Linear, entire, greyish leaves crowd the much-branched stems. Involucral bracts (in about 3 ranks) are green, with tips generally turned outward. This species is abundant in sandy soil, especially above the margins of alkaline ponds in the Dry Interior plains. Range: s. B.C. and Wash., e. of Cascades.

86. SPOTTED KNAPWEED,
Centaurea maculosa

This native of Europe is now well-established on roadsides and in waste places in s. B.C. and e. Wash., sporadic in s. Vancouver I. A biennial or short-lived perennial, its scraggly stems and narrowly-pinnate leaves are felted with grey hairs. Two to five feet in height, the numerous branches each end in a knob-like dark bud. These open from June to Oct., to reveal a head of purplish, deeply-cut, florets.

87 × 0.2

88 × 0.3

87. RABBIT BRUSH, *Chrysothamnus nauseosus*
Also known locally as 'False Goldenrod', this variable species averages 2' but may reach 6' high. The much-branched twigs are thin and wiry, closely covered with grey-green felted hairs, as are often the numerous linear leaves. Heads are usually 5-flowered; Aug.-Oct. Found mostly in dry open places in plains and foothills. Range: s. B.C. to n. Cal., generally e. of Cascades.

88. SLENDER HAWKSBEARD, *Crepis atrabarba*
This many-stemmed yellow-flowered perennial is conspicuous from May to July in dry open places in the mountains and valleys of s. B.C. and e. Wash., e. of Cascade summits. Smooth stems are branched near the top, and each branchlet is terminated by a flower-head about ¾" broad. Leaves are chiefly basal, and deeply pinnately-divided into very slender lobes. The thread-like pappus of the (usually) greenish achenes are fancied to be like the bristle-hairs about the beak of a hawk.

89. HOARY CHAENACTIS, *Chaenactis douglasii*

This variable 4-20" biennial is locally common on the arid plains of the Interior, to rather high elevations in the mountains. The erect plants, covered with white hairs, have deeply bipinnate leaves that are basal, and also alternate up the stem. Flower-heads are ½-¾" broad, bearing flesh-coloured (fading whitish) flowers from May to Sept. Range: s. B.C. to n. Cal., e. of Cascades.

90. COMMON SUNFLOWER, *Helianthus annuus*

An impressive annual, up to 7' high, which has ripened flower-heads (June-Sept.) as much as 5" across in the wild, though cultivated varieties far exceed this. Stems and 6-12" pointed-ovate leaves bear hairs stiff enough to puncture the skin. This native of N. America has been cultivated for centuries, and so it has become widespread beyond its natural range. It is common on roadsides and open places throughout the Dry Interior regions of the Pacific N.W.

× 0.2

× 0.3

91. HOOKER'S THISTLE,
Cirsium hookerianum

This short-lived perennial thistle is generally hoary with dense white hairs. Leaves have margins less deeply-toothed than most thistles, and moderately spiny. The flowers, creamy-white, have heads almost 2" wide. In July and Aug. this bold plant may be seen in bloom in moist bottom-lands and pockets of deeper soil, to moderate altitudes. Range: s. B.C. and n. Wash., e. of Cascades.

92. WAVY-LEAF THISTLE,
Cirsium undulatum

A tall biennial (occasionally 7') with stems covered with white hairs. Leaves, more deeply-toothed than **91**, are woolly-white on both sides, but in older leaves the upper surface becomes nearly smooth. Flower-heads (1½"-3" wide) are pale lavender to pinkish; May to Sept. A plant of the dry prairies and roadsides of s. B.C., n. Wash. and Ore., e. of Cascades.

93. SCABLAND FLEABANE,
Erigeron bloomeri
This tap-rooted perennial, much-branched at the base, has many narrow 2½"-long basal leaves covered in fine, white hairs. Yellow flower-heads are solitary on 5-6" stalks, appearing from June to Aug. Found in dry rocky places in mountains and foothills. Range: c. Wash. to n. Cal., e. of Cascades.

94 × 0·2

95 × 1·0

94. PALE EVERLASTING, *Antennaria umbrinella*
Very similar to **76** in its dwarf, mat-forming habit, and persistently grey-woolly foliage. The bracts are round-tipped and vary from brown to grey-green at the base, to grey-white at the tip. Flowering through the summer months throughout our range, according to elevation, this attractive species brightens rock ledges and crevices on mountains from low elevations where it integrates with **76**, to high elevations, integrating with *A. Alpina* (see Field guide 6, *Wild flowers of the mountains*).

95. LINE-LEAF FLEABANE, *Erigeron linearis*
This beautiful perennial species is abundant among the Sagebrush and up to moderate elevations in the mountains in s. B.C., Wash., and Ore., e. of Cascades. Large yellow flower-heads usually span 1″ or more. Nearly always they are solitary on a 2-12″ stem from May to July. The leaves, fleshy, long and linear (as the species name implies), are almost entirely basal. Leaves, stems, and involucral bracts are covered with short grey hairs.

96. CUSHION FLEABANE,
Erigeron poliospermus

A perennial, tap-rooted plant forming tufts of hairy linear leaves, less than 3" high. Solitary flower-heads about 1" wide have ray-florets that are pink, purple, or violet, enclosing a yellowish-green centre. Seen in late April to June in dry open places in Sagebrush areas. Range: s. B.C. to c. Ore., e. of Cascades.

97   × 0·2

98   × 0·2

97. SHAGGY FLEABANE, *Erigeron pumilus*
This abundant plant of the Sagebrush country is a much-branched perennial, often bushy in appearance. Numerous many-rayed flower-heads open from May to July. The rays may be white, or more rarely pinkish or bluish, stems, 2-16" tall, are covered (like the leaves and involucre) with spreading hairs. Involucral bracts are narrowly lanceolate, green with a brownish midrib. Range: s. B.C. and Wash., e. of Cascades.

98. HORSE BRUSH, *Tetradymia canescens*
Closely resembling **87** with which it often grows, Horse Brush is whitish rather than grey-green, and it has leaves which are wider and only half as long as Rabbit Brush. As the prefix 'Tetra' (four) implies, this plant has 4 yellow flowers in each flower-head. Like **87**, this is a much-branched shrub, 12-24" high, crowned with masses of golden-yellow flower-heads from June to Sept. Found in dry open places in lowlands and foothills. Range: s. B.C. to n. Cal., e. of Cascades.

99. BROWN-EYED SUSAN,
Gaillardia aristata

This perennial is one of our most handsome wild flowers. It is found in the less dry portions of the flat prairie, never climbing high into the mountains. The seldom-branched stems, about 10-24″ tall are somewhat grey-haired (like the leaves). Splendid terminal flower-heads may span as much as 3″. From May to September these striking golden blooms, with their orange-brown centres, make vivid patches of colour in the grey dusty landscape. Range: B.C. to n. Ore., mostly e. of Cascades.

100. RESIN-WEED,
Grindelia squarrosa

This is a biennial or short-lived perennial of dry open places from s.e. B.C. to n. Cal., e. of Cascades. The smooth stem (up to 30" tall) is clasped by oblong, gummy leaves. Showy yellow flower-heads, smaller than those of the coast species, rarely span 1½", appearing from July to Sept. The involucral bracts are all strongly reflexed, with the possible exception of the innermost row.

101 × 1·0

101. LIATRIS, *Liatris punctata*
This is a showy perennial about 1′ tall, with alternate linear leaves. Rather unusual flowerheads consist of about 5 pink-purple, long-tubular florets, each one 'perfect' (having both stamens and pistils), July-Sept. Found in dry open places in sandy soil, this variable species ranges mostly e. of the Rockies. However, it also occurs in the area of the Siskiyou mountains of s.w. Ore., and n.w. Cal. Known also as 'Blazing Star', this common name has been omitted in the heading to avoid confusion with **49.**

102. BLACK-EYED SUSAN,
Rudbeckia hirta

An attractive 12-30" tall biennial which has alternate, elliptical to lanceolate leaves, long-stalked at the base of the stem, but shorter-stalked and finally sessile upward. Showy single flower-heads are often 3" across. The bright yellow ray florets are effectively accented by the rounded, central boss of almost black disk-flowers; June-Aug. Native to c. U.S.A., it has become established in open dry places throughout the Pacific N.W. (Reported on Vancouver I.)

103. DWARF GOLDENROD,
Solidago spathulata

This highly variable plant may not exceed 3" in poor soil and foot-hill situations, but often reaches 1-2' in Dry Interior regions. In its various forms this 'Goldenrod' ranges throughout the Pacific N.W. in a wide variety of habitats from sea level to subalpine and alpine levels. The inflorescence is usually dense, each yellow flower-head consisting of 8 ray- and 12-13 disk-florets; June-Sept.

Index

Agoseris glauca 77
Amsinckia intermedia 63
Anchusa officinalis 62
Antennaria rosea 76
   umbrinella 94
Arctium lappa 78
   minus 78
Arnica fulgens 79
Arrow-leaf Balsam-root 83
Artemisia frigida 80
   tridentata 81
Asclepias speciosa 55
Aster pansus 85
Astragalus miser 33

Baby's Breath 11
Balsamorhiza hookeri 82
   sagittata 83
Big-headed Clover 40
Bitter Root 14
Black-eyed Susan 102
Blazing Star 49, 101
Blue Clematis 16
Brittle Prickly Pear 47
Brown-eyed Susan 99

California Hesperochiron 66
Calochortus macrocarpus 1
Castilleja sulphurea 70
Ceanothus velutinus 45
Centaurea maculosa 86
Chaenactis douglasii 89
Choke Cherry 28
Chrysopsis villosa 84
Chrysothamnus
   nauseosus 87
Cirsium hookerianum 91
   undulatum 92
Clarkia pulchella 38
Clematis columbiana 16
   ligusticifolia 13
Cleome lutea 22
Common Anchusa 62
   Hound's Tongue 67
   Mullein 71
   Sagebrush 81
   Saxifrage 23
   Sunflower 90
Convolvulus arvensis 56
Corydalis aurea 18
Coryphantha vivipara 46
Crepis atrabarba 88
Cushion Coryphantha 46
   Fleabane 96
Cynoglossum officinale 67

Descurainia sophia 20
Douglas' Buckwheat 6
Dwarf Goldenrod 103
   Hesperochiron 66

Elaeagnus commutata 50
Erigeron bloomeri 93
   linearis 95
   poliospermus 96
   pumilus 97
Eriogonum compositum 5
   douglasii 6
   flavum 7
   umbellatum 9
Evening Primrose 51

Fall Dandelion 77
False Dandelion 77
   Goldenrod 87
Fiddle-neck 63
Field Bindweed 56
Flixweed 20
Fritillaria pudica 2

Gaillardia aristata 99
Gairdner's Penstemon 73
Geranium viscosissimum 42
Geum triflorum 26
Gilia aggregata 57
Golden Aster 84
   Corydalis 18
Greasewood 30
Great Burdock 78
Grindelia squarrosa 100
Gromwell 68
Gypsophila paniculata 11

Hedysarum
   sulphurescens 36
Helianthus annuus 90
Hesperochiron
   californicus 66
   pumilus 66
Heuchera cylindrica 19
Hoary Chaenactis 89
Hooker's Balsam-root 82
   Thistle 91
Horse Brush 98

Indian Wheat 75

Large-fruit Lomatium 53
Late Yellow Locoweed 37
Leafy Lungwort 69
Leptodactylon pungens 58

Lesser Burdock 78
Lewisia rediviva 14
   tweedyi 15
Liatris 101
Liatris punctata 101
Lilium philadelphicum 4
   washingtonianum 3
Line-leaf Fleabane 95
Linum perenne 41
Lithospermum ruderale 68
Lomatium macrocarpum 53
Long-leaved Phlox 61
Lungwort 69
Lupinus sericeus 34

Many-spined Prickly
   Pear 48
Mariposa Lily 1
Mentzelia laevicaulis 49
Mertensia longiflora 69
   oblongifolia 69

Narrow-leaved Phacelia 65
Northern Buckwheat 5

Oenothera biennis 51
   pallida 52
Onobrychis viciaefolia 35
Opuntia fragilis 47
   polyacantha 48
Oxytropis campestris 37
   splendens 39

Pale Agoseris 77
   Everlasting 94
Pallid Paintbrush 70
Pasture Sage 80
   Wormwood 80
Penstemon fruticosus var.
   scouleri 72
   gairdneri 73
   rydbergii 74
Periwinkle Phlox 60
Phacelia heterophylla 64
   linearis 65
Phlox adsurgens 60
   caespitosa 59
   longifolia 61
Pink Fairies 38
   Oenothera 52
   Pussy-toes 76
Plantago patagonica 75
   purshii 75
Poison Ivy 43

Potentilla fruticosa 27
   glandulosa 29
Prunus virginiana 28
Purple Avens 26
Purshia tridentata 30
Pussy-paws 8
Pyramid spiraea 32

Rabbit Brush 87
Ranunculus glaberrimus 17
Red Glasswort 10
Resin-weed 100
Rhododendron
   occidentale 54
Rhus glabra 44
   radicans 43
Ribes cereum 24
   viscosissimum 25
Rosa woodsii 31
Round-leaved Alumroot 19
Rudbeckia hirta 102
Rydberg's Penstemon 74

Sagebrush Buttercup 17
Salicornia rubra 10
Salsola kali 12

Sandfain 35
Saxifraga bronchialis 23
Scabland Fleabane 93
Scarlet Gilia 57
Shaggy Fleabane 97
Shining Arnica 79
Showy Milkweed 55
   Oxytropis 39
Shrubby Cinquefoil 27
   Penstemon 72
Silky Lupine 34
Silver-berry 50
Sisymbrium altissimum 21
Slender Hawksbeard 88
Snowbrush 45
Solidago spathulata 103
Spiny Phlox 58
Spiraea pyramidata 32
Spotted Knapweed 86
Spraguea umbellata 8
Squaw Currant 24
Sticky Cinquefoil 29
   Currant 25
   Geranium 42
Sulphur Flower 9
Sumac 44

Tetradymia canescens 98
Trifolium
   macrocephalum 40
Tufted Phlox 59
   White Prairie Aster 85
Tumblemustard 21
Tumbleweed 12
Tweedy's Lewisia 15

Varied-leaved Phacelia 64
Verbascum thapsus 71

Washington Lily 3
Wavy-leaf Thistle 92
Weedy Milk Vetch 33
Western Azalea 54
White Virgin's Bower 13
Wild Blue Flax 41
Wood Lily 4
Wood's Rose 31

Yellow Bell 2
   Buckwheat 7
   Loments 36
   Spiderflower 22

Glossary

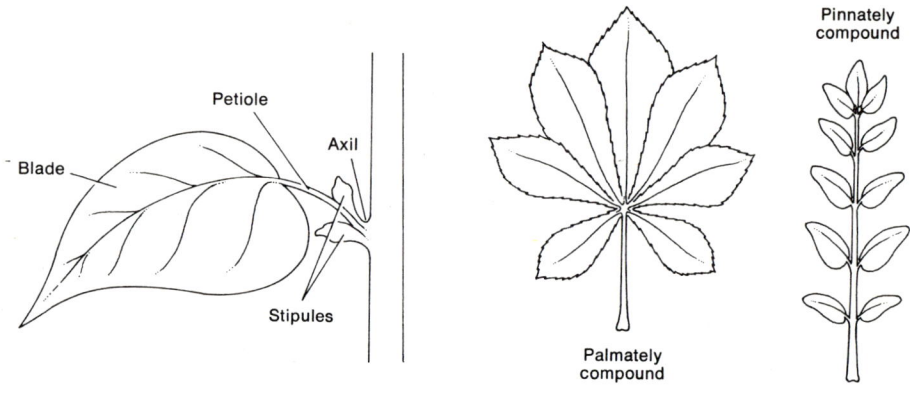

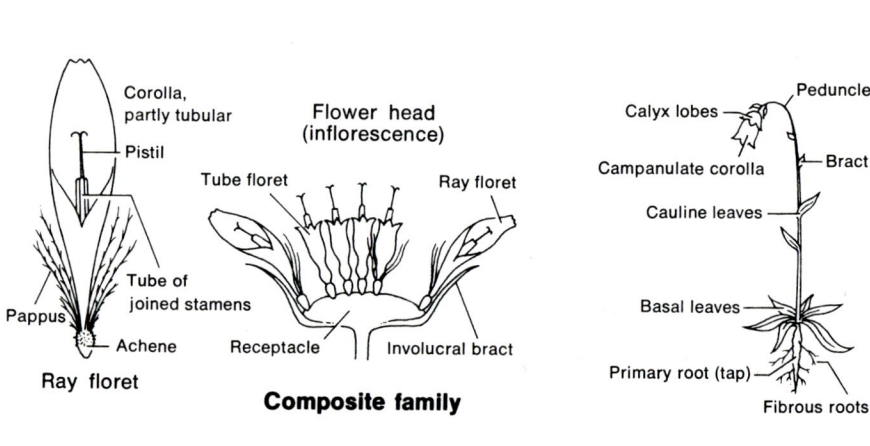

Figures in blue under each picture in the book indicate the scale of the reproduction, e.g. ×0·5 means the picture is half as large as the actual (average) plant; ×2·0 means the picture is twice as large as the plant.

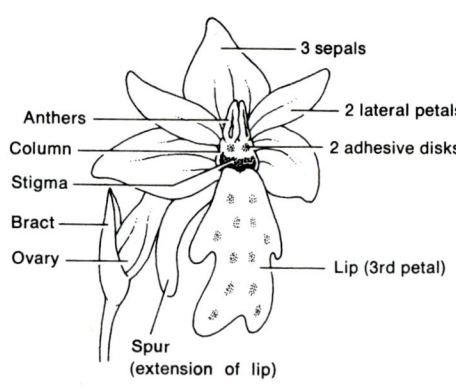